MORE MEMORIES OF
BLACKBURN

TRUE NORTH BOOKS
DEAN CLOUGH
HALIFAX,
WEST YORKSHIRE HX3 5AX
TEL 01422 344344

THE PUBLISHERS WOULD LIKE TO THANK THE
FOLLOWING COMPANIES FOR SUPPORTING THE
PRODUCTION OF THIS BOOK

MAIN SPONSOR
CAVALIER CARPETS LIMITED

TOMMY BALL (SUPPLIES) LIMITED

BRITISH AEROSPACE MILITARY AIRCRAFT
AND AEROSTRUCTURES

BRITISH AEROSPACE ROYAL ORDNANCE PLC

GEORGE BROUGHTON & COMPANY LIMITED

THE CHERRY TREE MACHINE COMPANY LIMITED

COBBLE (BLACKBURN) LIMITED

SANDERSONS CONFECTIONERS

WESTHOLME SCHOOL LIMITED

WHALLEYS HULTON & PROCTOR (BLACKBURN) LIMITED

First published in Great Britain by True North Books
Dean Clough
Halifax HX3 5AX
1998

© TRUE NORTH HOLDINGS
ISBN 1 900 463 96 2

Introduction

Montague Street during the late 1940s.

Welcome to *More Memories of Blackburn,* a look back at some of the places, events and people in the area which have shaped the lives of local people over a period of around half a century. The following pages are brought to life by a selection of images from the not-too-distant past, chosen according to their ability to rekindle memories of days gone by and showing how people used to shop, work and play in the area where they grew up. Modern image reproduction techniques have enabled us to present these pictures in a way rarely seen before and the lively design and informative text attempts to create a collection of Blackburn images that readers will treasure for many years to come.

This is not a book about crinolines or bowler-hats. Neither is *More Memories of Blackburn* a work of local history in the normal sense of the term. It is hoped that the following pages will revive pleasant memories of Blackburn from days gone by. Scenes featuring the extremes of the weather experienced over the years are included, along with pictures relating to shopping, celebrating public events and relaxing in the town. Some delightful pictures of Her Majesty Queen Elizabeth are shown when she visited the town in the 1950s.

George Formby makes an appearance as does the Rt. Hon. Baroness of Blackburn, the former Barbara Castle M.P. Several of Blackburn Rovers' outstanding personalities and players from days gone by are featured along with action shots and information from some of the more memorable matches they played.

Many local companies and organisations have allowed us to study their archives and include their history here- and fascinating reading it makes too. The present-day guardians of the firms concerned are proud of their products, the achievements of their people and the hard work of their forefathers whose efforts created these long-established organisations. We are pleased to make it possible for them to share their history with a wider audience.

When we began compiling *More Memories of Blackburn* several months ago we anticipated that the task would be a pleasurable one, but our expectations were greatly surpassed. There is a growing appetite for all things 'nostalgic' and we are pleased that this book will swell the number of images and associated information available to the growing number of nostalgia enthusiasts.

Happy memories!

CONTENTS

Events & occasions

Bearing a striking resemblance to our own Prince Charles, the Duke of Kent visited Blackburn in July 1938. This picture shows the popular Duke chatting informally to a group gathered outside Carr's Mill before getting back into his gleaming black Rolls Royce. Ladies, all wearing hats of course, can be seen straining to catch every word uttered by the Duke, and one young lady keeps a firm hand on the arm of her daughter as the distinguished figure moves along the line of well-wishers. At the time this picture was taken the storm clouds were gathering over Europe. The lives of all the people in this picture would soon be changed forever.

Utter devastation was caused by a German bomb which exploded in the Ainsworth Street area in August 1940. The enemy raider had dropped his explosive cargo at 1.43 p.m on the 31st August and the properties shown here had suffered the brunt of the damage. Windows were shattered in an extensive area around the blast area causing temendous inconvenience and misery. The shop owned and run by William Charnley can be seen in the centre of the picture, bloodied but unbowed by the Nazi raiders. Passers-by scrutinised the damage along the normally-busy street, their sense of shock and disbelief being apparent as the War arrives on their doorstep. Two soldiers, probably members of the Home Guard, were detailed to stand guard on the street. Not that there was much likelihood of looting being a problem as the community pulled together in the aftermath of the attack.

Above: A rather youthful looking Barbara Castle makes her bid for a seat in the House of Commons in 1945. Her subsequent success resulted in her serving the town for over thirty years and the quality of her contribution to British politics led to a well deserved seat in the House of Lords. The July 1945 election saw Labour returned with a landslide victory, winning 393 seats to the Conservative Party's 199. Attlee had been the leader of the Labour Party since 1935 and this resounding victory was the first time Labour had been returned with an independent majority. A few days after this picture was taken the newspaper headlines described a dramatic accident in the USA in which a massive B25 bomber crashed into the Empire State Building. Thirteen people died and 26 were seriously injured in the tragedy.

Top: 'Turned out nice again, hasn't it?' And it certainly had on the day that George Formby visited the Town Hall to attend a Civic reception in his honour in February 1942. He is seen here with his characteristic beaming smile, part of the package which made him the most popular male personality in Britain from the late 1930s to the mid 1940s. Formby was born in the nearby town of Wigan and, like his equally popular contemporary star Gracie Fields, he never lost his thick local accent or sight of his Lancashire roots. Both were national stars in their own right, working class heroes of the masses who created a much needed sense of cheerfulness and optimism among the audiences which flocked to see them.

Lancashire Evening Telegraph

Local mothers pulled out all the stops to put on this fine street party spread for the children in the neighbourhood in June 1953. The celebration was held to mark the coronation of Queen Elizabeth and it would have rekindled memoris of the last street parties to be held in the area. That was at the end of the Second World War, when the celebrations were conducted amid thoughts of the suffering that had

been endured by the population for a six year period. Most of the children in this picture were born at around the time that the war had ended and it is certain that they would have ben familiar with the rationing and shortages which went hand in hand with this era. Indeed, rationing affected the supply of many products right up until 1954. This picture was taken in Montague Street.

Above: A stirring sight dating from 1940 which features the Town Hall during War Weapons Week. The fund-raising event took place in December and was designed to encourage people to lend their savings to the government for the war effort. War Bonds, Defence Bonds and Savings Certificates could be bought and the total was displayed on this 'thermometer' at the Town Hall as well as in reports in local daily papers. The campaign was launched by Major Walter Elliot and went on to raise over one million pounds.

Top: Victory at last. There was cause for widespread celebration and thanksgiving when the news broke that the Germans had surrendered in 1945. On May 4th 1945 Field Marshal Montgomery accepted the surrender of the German forces in the Netherlands, north Germany and Denmark. The official end of the conflict occurred on May 7th with the signing of the unconditional surrender of all German forces. May 8th was declared a public holiday to be known as Victory in Europe Day. Parades and street parties were held all over Britain. There were fireworks displays, dancing in the streets, religious ceremonies of thanksgiving and rallies in the parks. All this was, of course, tinged with sadness and thoughts of those who would not be coming back from the war. Most families had suffered a loss of this kind and no one who lived through the conflict could ever be the same again, no matter how much they wanted to be.

Left: Wings for Victory campaigns were held throughout Britain during 1943 to raise money to purchase military aircraft. Members of the public would buy bonds or donate money to the campaign and the daily amounts raised would be publicised in local papers, set against local targets and the amounts raised in neighbouring towns. This picture shows No. 1 Company of the Home Guard as it marches past the General Post Office in Darwen Street. The campaign for victory through air power was well underway when this picture was taken.

Lancashire Evening Telegraph

Above: Many people will remember the widespread flooding which devastated Blackburn, Darwen and the surrounding district in 1964. Wakes Week was particularly badly affected by the rising waters and the shops and residents of Princess Street and the Waterfall area had their properties severely damaged. Fire and Police personnel were called in to evacuate residents in the most badly affected areas. This photograph shows an experienced police sergeant demonstrating the correct way to carry a pretty young lady to the safety of a waiting lorry. No doubt the young policeman would get a chance to practice this new skill on several large, elderly gentlemen in the houses down the street!

Left: An historic photograph taken to record the last journey to be made on the Blackburn Corporation tramcar system. Corporation officials, looking rather *starchy* as a result of either the autumn weather or the demands of the photographer, can be seen standing beside the last vehicle to be used on the very last journey. The picture was taken on September 3rd 1949 before the tram set off from the Boulevard on the Intack route. Thousands of people lined the roads to cheer and wave at the vehicle and its passengers, symbolising the end of an era which had lasted more than half a century.

Above: A series of events guaranteed to appeal to everyone in Blackburn took place in August and September 1951. The cause of the celebrations was the town's 100th anniversary of its incorporation as a Borough. This huge banner was displayed at the railway station, but the town and the local newspaper carried huge amounts of publicity material to ensure that nobody could miss the events. The railway station itself had only recently celebrated its centenary, having been opened to the public in 1848. An interesting range of publications was available at the *Finlays* news kiosk on the left, ranging from the *Radio Times* with its 'look before you listen' slogan, to *Photoplay* in which readers could 'meet the stars from the silver screen' for 1/3d per month.

"BLACKBURN CELEBRATED 100 YEARS AS A BOROUGH IN AUGUST AND SEPTEMBER 1951"

Centenary Year.
E SHOW
OWLS • FIREWORKS DISPLAY
LA DAY • HALLE ORCHESTRA
AL BALL • DANCES
s Aug. — Sept. 1951
SHOPPING FESTIVAL WEEK.
OPEN AIR
MERRIE ENGLAND
ATHLETIC SPORTS. CYCLE HILL CLIMB
Marionettes

Below: Was this downtown Blackburn or a scene from the Swiss Alps we wonder? The presence of the Lord Nelson pub at the end of Penney Street and the co-operative policeman in his waterproof white coat suggest that it was, in fact, Blackburn. The picture was taken to illustrate the extent of the wintry weather in 1963 for an article in the *Lancashire Evening Telegraph*. Normally of course, the police officer's white coat would have made him more visible to passing traffic as he performed point-duty. The bright white coat would have had the opposite effect on this snow-covered day - but thankfully there were few vehicles around to pose a danger to him.

This scene dates from the late 1950s and shows a procession of young girls making their way through Blackburn town centre, past the Royal Cinema and towards the Wilpshire bus terminus on the right of the picture. The street is lined with well-wishers and relatives cheering and clapping their appreciation as the proud youngsters passed by. Just out of shot a banner indicates an association with the Church of the Saviour and across the way the local cinema advertises Botany Bay starring alan Ladd and James Mason. Above that advertising banner the words 'Long Live the Queen' are displayed.

The Coronation of Her Majesty Queen Elizabeth II took place on June 2nd 1953. Blackburn, in common with hundreds of towns throughout Britain, entered into the spirit of the occasion with lavish decorations throughout the town as well virtually every place of employment in the area. Flags and bunting added a sense of excitement to mills such as this one, though modern-day safety inspectors would rightly complain about the fire risk they posed. People throughout the land were genuinely thrilled and enthralled by the coronation. There was a tremendous sense of loyalty to the Crown and this was reflected in the crowds which turned out to watch the procession to and from Westminster Abbey. It was estimated that 30,000 people camped out overnight in the Mall in order to secure a good view of the proceedings. In Blackburn, anyone with a television suddenly found scores of new friends, all eager to spend the day of the coronation in front of the tiny screen with them. In Britain as a whole two and a half million T.V sets were being used to watch the event and this boosted demand for the new medium tremendously.

Lancashire Evening Telegraph

This breathtaking picture shows King William Street as never been seen before - or since. For days before the 1955 visit of the Queen and Duke of Edinburgh the whole town had buzzed with excitement. Civic leaders had made extensive preparations for the arrival of the royal couple and military personnel had rehearsed their drills for the ceremony endlessly. It had seemed as if the whole town had turned out to greet the royal party, the cheering was deafening and the air full of red, white and blue flags waving in a vast display of loyalty and affection for the monarch. On the right of this picture, against the wall of the old Town Hall the specially-constructed stand can be seen which provided a grandstand view and reassuring shelter for V.I.Ps from Blackburn and neighbouring towns.

Above: Looking radiant and stylishly dressed the young Queen Elizabeth is introduced to local Church leaders as part of her visit in 1955. Waiting, no doubt slightly apprehensively, was Blackburn's local hero and proud Victoria Cross holder Mr N. Grimbaldeston.

Left: The moment at which the Regimental Colours were presented to the Queen when she came to Blackburn in 1955. All this took place on the forecourt area of the old Town Hall in full view of hundreds of V.I.P guests (seated in the special stand) and thousands of Blackburn folk who had travelled into town for the occasion. Four or five old fashioned invalid carriages can be seen just a few paces from where the Queen was standing. These particular vehicles were driven by war veterans - real V.I.Ps in their own right, who were introduced to Her Majesty. It is always interesting to compare the level of 'royal' security in old photographs like this. In modern times, for instance, it would be unusual for the group of photographers (seen next to the invalid carriages) to be allowed to stand so close to the monarch.

Above: Part of the itinerary for the 1955 royal visit included a tour around the Baird works in Blackburn. Her Majesty is seen emerging from the factory into the bright sunshine with the local director in charge of the company. Two policemen are in view, providing reassuring, but largely unnecessary security for the royal party. The newly-polished medals worn so proudly by the police officers remind us that the Second War had ended less than ten years earlier. Their smart white gloves are evidence of an era when cleanliness was considered to be next to Godliness. It was a time before graffiti covered our bus shelters and park benches, (indeed, *graffiti* was not a commonly used term in the 1950s), and a time when wayward youngsters took real notice of a stern look from a vigilant Bobby.

Right: The Queen is seen here outside the old Town Hall as Regimental Colours were being presented by the Guard of Honour. It was April 1955. A few days earlier the Prime Minister, Winston Churchill resigned due to ill health and was succeeded by Anthony Eden.

Bright sunshine and a light breeze provided the background for the visit of Her Majesty the Queen and the Duke of Edinburgh in April 1955. In this picture Her Majesty is about to inspect the Guard of Honour accompanied by their Commanding Officer and followed by the Duke of Edinburgh and other members of the royal party. In the distance the Westminster Bank had set a high standard for the royal decorations in the town centre, a standard which scores of other firms tried hard to match. This was 1955, the year that another member of the royal family, Princess Margaret, was being wooed by Group Captain Peter Townsend, causing intense speculation in the press. In turn this rekindled unpleasant memories of the 1935 abdication crisis of the then Edward VIII and the American divorcee Mrs Wallace Simpson. Ultimately the princess announced that she would not marry the Group Captain after being compelled to choose between her royal duty and her own happiness.

Top right: Standing upright for the National Anthem, Her Majesty the Queen, the Duke of Edinburgh and Brigadier J.M. Hepper. This was a proud moment for the townspeople of Blackburn who gave a rousing welcome to the popular royal couple. The picture dates from 14th April 1955, less than two years after the coronation in Westminster Abbey. There were many memorable events from this year; only four days after this picture was taken Albert Einstein, the most famous scientist of all time, died in America.

Three months after the picture was taken Ruth Ellis was executed after being convicted for murdering her lover, David Blakely. Good news for people in Blackburn, and most other industrial towns, came in the form of the Clean Air Act, passed in 1955 after the devastating smog which caused thousands of deaths in 1952.

Right: The distinctive white tiles of the Royal Cinema can be seen in the background of this picture as Corporation workmen put the final touches to decorations for the 1953 Coronation. Towns and cities throughout the country were lavishly decorated for the coronation of Her Majesty Queen Elizabeth II when it took place in Westminster Abbey. Street parties, dances, processions and concerts were organised - it was the first real chance for the nation to celebrate after the end of the Second World War.

Cavalier Carpets - a craft that became an industry

Carpets were a craft long before they became an industry. Nowhere is that better known than in England's northern mill towns. Establishing a carpet company in Blackburn, a town where spinning and weaving are in the blood, was not a task to be taken lightly. However, it was well within the capacities of Mr Gerry Lowe, its present managing director.

His early career involved working for himself selling carpets on market stalls throughout the country. Based in Hollins Grove Street, Darwen, Lancashire, his business grew to such an extent that he was soon able to establish a wholesale operation, manufacturing carpets on commission.

Cavalier Carpets was established in 1974 and commenced operations in a somewhat less than prestigious factory. The commission side of Gerry Lowe's business mushroomed and a link was forged with Cavalier Carpets which led to the present scenario. Since then the company has never looked back.

Its first ten years was a period of ever-increasing turnover, from just over half a million in the first year to more than fourteen million pounds in the tenth. In 1979 a move was made to Anchor Mill in Moss Fold Road, Darwen.

Later, additional premises were found at Bank Top Mill in Thompson Street Industrial Estate in Blackburn. Later still, Burns Mill, Selous Road, Blackburn was acquired.

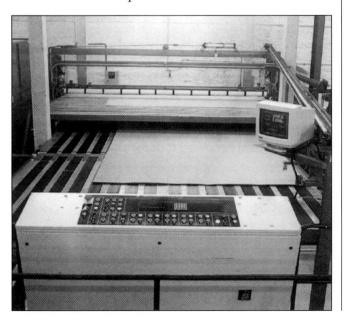

> "IN 1979 A MOVE WAS MADE TO ANCHOR MILL IN MOSS FOLD ROAD, DARWEN"

Just recently a fourth operational site was opened at Shadwell Industrial Estate, also in Blackburn.

Above: Workers in the Axminster manufacturing area.
Left: A computer aids the process of cutting lengths.
Facing page, bottom: The Cavalier Carpets showroom in the 1980s.
Facing page, top right: One of the QE2's cabins, with carpet supplied by the company.
Facing page, top left: Gerry Lowe, managing director of Cavalier Carpets.

became the largest users of wool in the British tufted carpet industry.

In 1984 Tony Bell became the company's UK sales director. Under his guidance Cavalier widened its customer base. Previously a large percentage of sales were to the large groups which had a firm grip on the market. It became deliberate company policy to sell to the small but numerous independents as well as to large multiples.

The strategy for the early years was devoted to the retail market, making tufted carpets in various fibres and this resulted in steady, sustained growth.

The company was once advised, 'Never argue about taste,'. Its designers therefore endeavoured to satisfy the mainstream demand but not at the expense of new and innovative trends.

The first wool carpet had been produced in 1980 and then, in 1982, business expanded dramatically when Cavalier decided to make a move to the top end of the market by establishing links with the wool producers, introducing wool and wool-blend carpets into its ranges. The company quickly

Dieter Jolmes, export and contract director was also enlarging the company's global markets and 1986 saw Cavalier expanding from the domestic into the contract market, an area where it soon

Above: HRH the Duchess of Kent presenting a British Wool Marketing Board woven carpet Quality award to Gerry Lowe in 1994.
Right: The company's warehouse which carries 2,800 rolls of carpet.
Facing page, top: A charity tea party held by the company raised £10,000 for Children in Need.
Facing page, centre: The mainframe computer in the 1980s.
Facing page, bottom: The factory in 1980.

special healthcare carpet, Cavalshield' to meet the demand from both public and private healthcare customers.

There was a boom in new building and refurbishment in the eighties which was a great asset to Cavalier's eager contract sales team. However, the company had the wisdom to keep its market hold in retail, export

established itself both at home and overseas. First steps were tentative but soon trade in this area was flourishing. Custom made carpets were supplied to hotels, hospitals, banks and other commercial interiors. An early job was to supply carpeting for the huge Mount Pleasant Post Office in central London.

Competition was fierce and new lines were continually introduced to meet new market requirements. For example, Cavalier designed and made a

and contract and this policy saw it safely through the difficult recessionary years.

This rapid development was realised by massive investment in plant, machinery and the very latest that technology had to offer. An innovation in the early eighties was the introduction of a computerised graphics machine. It was new in carpet technology, using microchips to produce patterned carpeting which previously had only been available to makers of woven carpets.

Now the company could manufacture top quality carpet in a fraction of the time and at a fraction of the cost of traditional carpets. Using microchips instead of Jacquard pattern cards brought the opulence of the finest woven carpets well within the budget of the average homelover for the first time.

The present design studio at Cavalier has all the very latest technology to produce intricate design and colour schemes efficiently and quickly. It is staffed by experienced designers who will produce ideas for customers or transform customers' own ideas into reality, producing a beautiful carpet that is perfect for the required location.

Other purchases around the same time were the mainframe computer to streamline administration and new high speed machinery to replace the old tufting machines. A new autowrap and pack machine meant better presentation of finished carpet. The purchase of a new 105,000 square feet warehouse had an adjacent prestige office complex.

The introduction of Axminster carpets in 1992 put Cavalier in a stronger position in both retail and contract business. At that time sales were predominantly retail, at approximately 50% with 25% of production for contract and 25% for export.

Above: In 1995 Cavalier won Exporter of the Year award.
Left: Tufted production at Cavalier is extensive. The company currently has nine tufting machines.

marine companies, Cavalier have supplied Cunard, P & O, Sealink, Chios Marine (a Greek company) and MV Fairwinds (a West Indian one). Cavalier's Far East links include carpets laid in Beijing Airport and the world famous Mandarin and Park Lane Hotels in Hong Kong. The company's foothold in this part of the world will hopefully grow from this kind of initiative.

Cavalier is known for its ability to challenge time scales and fulfil orders other manufacturers turn down. It is a company

One of the many prestigious installations included the QE2 liner, where Cavalier supplied the main bulk of custom designed carpets which were fitted in premium, deluxe and super-deluxe cabins. The carpeting was designed by Cavalier Carpets and featured an over-all multi pin dot pattern in different colourways to blend with other cabin furnishings.

Other Cavalier products have been used widely to furnish other ships and their Monmartre collection has attained the standards set by the International Maritime Organisation's fire test procedures. The carpets in the collection have a low flame spread and have been awarded the IMO classification granted to a select number only. Amongst other

determined to go from strength to strength, its success firmly based on huge investment in plant machinery and each last piece of high technology that becomes available. With the addition of Wilton manufacturing in 1996, Cavalier are now one of the few manufacturers who can offer specialist Wilton, Axminster and tufted carpeting for all types of installations, be it domestic, contract or export. This flexibility is ensuring the company's continued success.

Top: Company horse Princess is first past the finishing post.
Above: The QE2. Cavalier supplied carpets for many of the cabins.
Left: The firm's main premises in 1988.

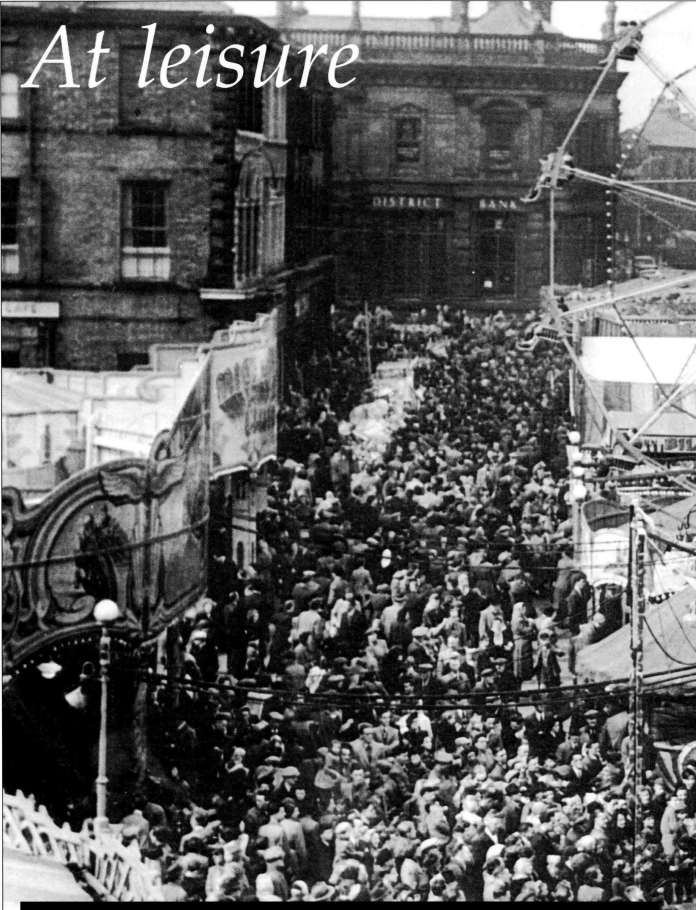

At leisure

A crowded scene in the town centre when the fair came to town in the early 1960s. In the distance, on the right, the white stone facade of the Burton's building can be seen with the District Bank building across the way on the left of it. The photograph is dominated by the Big Wheel, and those brave enough to take a ride on the flimsy structure would have gained an unrivalled view of the adjacent shops and streets. The last Easter Fair to be held in the Market Place was in 1964.

Lancashire Evening Telegraph

Above: A visit to Blackburn's fair was an exciting outing at any age and at any time of day. But after dark it was recognised that this was the domain of teenagers and young courting couples who could endure the noise and bright lights more comfortably than their younger (or older, come to that) contemporaries. It was an exciting place to be for the youngsters who had been trusted with an evening's freedom, particularly if this was their first unaccompanied visit to the fair. Parents would, for the most part, spend the evening fretting at home until their offspring returned. The bright lights attracted people from many miles around Blackburn, willing to spend a few shillings on the kind of entertainment you simply couldn't get anywhere else. Easter Fairs were held in Blackburn for a 112 year period between 1852 and 1964. Their initial purpose was closely linked to market trading, with sideshows for entertainment running alongside. Eventually the 'entertainment' side of the fair completely took over resulting in the kind of attraction depicted in this photograph.

Top: Blackburn's Easter Fair is featured in this picture from March 1956. The Big Wheel looks rather fragile compared to some modern-day attractions, but it always had a steady stream of customers eager to gain a birds-eye view of the town centre streets from the creaking seats. There seems hardly room to walk around the stalls and rides, huddled as they were against the wall of the old market building. It is nice to see the market clock tower, an icon of Blackburn's market trading activity if ever there was one. The distinctive white facade of the Burton's building dominates the background of the picture along with the Marks and Spencer store to the right of it.

Above: The Duttons Brewery annual staff outing to Blackpool
was an exercise in male/female segregation when this picture was taken in the late 1950s. The ladies not only
travelled on separate coaches but stayed in different hotels to the gents, some miles apart, in fact! Two of the
drivers are shown in their white jackets badged with the logo of Ribblesdale Batty-Holt. A variety of period
hairstyles, most involving Brylcreem, are in evidence.
Inset: This picture was taken shortly after the male Duttons contingent arrived in Blackpool. A few drinks were
certain to get them in the mood for the day ahead - and judging by some of the glum faces shown here it would
have taken quite a few bevvies to get the men in the holiday spirit.

An impressive series of public events and celebrations were organised by the Council to celebrate 100 years of Blackburn's local government status as a Borough. Pictured here are some of the prize winners at the Centenary Fancy Dress competition in 1951. This was the year of the Festival of Britain, held on a reclaimed bomb site on London's South Bank, exactly 100 years after the Great Exhibition of 1851. Critics said that the country could ill afford the £8 million cost of the exhibition. Their argument was overshadowed by the sense of optimism and confidence that the event created, but opponents pointed to the rationing of some products, which had remained in place so long after the end of the war, to support their view. A fact illustrated by a beef shortage during 1951 which resulted in the consumption of over 50,000 horses in Britain.

"WORKERS PLAYTIME WAS A POPULAR FAVOURITE ON THE 'WIRELESS' IN THE 1930s AND 1940s..."

Above: This charming picture show children of Furthergate School in the 1950-1 school year. The children shown are: (Front row) Joyce Heath, Carol Cooper, Carol Cornthwaite. (Second row) Carol Ireland, Mavis Deardon, Carol Selby, Marilyn Bannerman, Christine Cornthwaite, Margaret (?) and Pauline Watson. (Third row) Douglas Dawson, Jack Kay, Robert Houghton, Norman Adcroft, Ian Moore, Stephen Talbot, Gordon Greenhalgh, Ian Perkins, Fred Bates, Barry Rayton and John A.Brooks. (Back row) David Powney, Michael Timmins, Robert Morris, Alan Howarth, Graham Milligan, Brian Dawson, Alec Carmichael, Tom Sharples and Gordon Blake.

Below: *Workers Playtime* was a popular favourite on the wireless in the 1930s and 40s. Honesty compels us to say that we can't say *for sure* that this scene depicts the travelling radio show at a local factory canteen - but we think it does. The format of the programme was very progressive for its day. Talented workers at the factories concerned would be invited to do a 'turn' and a guest celebrity would make sure that the proceedings went with a swing. *Workers Playtime* was similar to modern day radio 'roadshows' in as much as the programme appealed to young people who looked forward to it visiting their town. Factory managers would undertake extensive preparations for the B.B.C's visit and the whole affair would receive extensive coverage in the local press.

Lancashire Evening Telegraph

A very respectable crowd, in every sense of the word, had gathered for this concert in Corporation Park in the 1920s. Respectability began with the wearing of a hat at the time this picture was taken, and you would struggle to find a member of this audience without one. The bandstand had been erected in September 1909 and could seat a considerable audience of 2000. It provided a very popular way of passing a few hours in the open air, listening to the music played by a variety of accomplished musicians. Some of the events from 1909 give an impression of what life was like for people in those days. January 1909 saw the payment of pensions to all British people over the age of 70 and in April that year the first double decker buses to run on British roads were introduced. Back on the subject of entertainment, Benny Goodman the US jazzman was born in this year, as was Katherine Hepburn, star of stage and screen.

Lancashire Evening Telegraph

Above: Long before the days of *Oasis* and the *Bay City Rollers* the blood pressure of most healthy young ladies could be raised by the presence of a singer from the popular group known as *The Four Pennies.* This popular chap was the lead singer from the group and is seen doing his best to sign scores of autographs for his excited young fans. The picture was taken in 1966 outside Lionel Morton's new Boutique *The Inn Place.*

Left: The *Locarno Ballroom* was a popular venue for trendy young people, all eager have a dance and mingle with members of the opposite sex, when this picture was taken in 1962. Countless numbers of local people met their eventual marital partners at venues such as this one, twisting, jiving or bopping away the evening to the latest popular music. 'Let's Twist Again' was a hit for the 20-year-old rising star Chubby Checker in the year that this picture was taken. The song immediately became the theme for the *Twist* - a dance which was performed by bending the knees and twisting from side to side on the balls of the feet, either with a partner or without one. People who were young in the 1960s can often be seen today doing the Twist at weddings and family get-togethers, much to the embarrassment of their younger relatives and friends.

Around the town centre

A 1927 picture of the Boulevard area with several interesting features from daily life at the time clearly in view. Despite the fact that car ownership was at a low level - or maybe because of it - around six cabs can be seen plying for trade. This could be holiday time, as several open-topped charas are neatly parked up on the left hand side of the picture.

At the period this picture was taken the main method

of public transport was the tramway network. By 1929 the introduction of motorbus services had taken place and the writing was on the wall for trams. The charas featured in this picture were the favoured method of recreational transport, making regular trips to the coast at annual and public holiday times. The white building in the picture, towards the right of the scene, is the cab-man's shelter.

You can almost sense the tension felt by the motorists as they squeeze their way down Northgate. They would have been used to hold-ups in the 1960s and this was at least part of the reason for the town centre redevelopment which took place here after this time. It was all part of a process which saw residential dwellings, usually of very poor quality, cleared from the 'inner' area, and ring roads and by-passes constructed to separate the local traffic from the vehicles which were simply 'passing through' en-route to distant destinations. The idea was to speed the flow of traffic and segregate shoppers from the smoky, dangerous vehicles which had previously competed with them for space in the middle of our towns. Several historic buildings were sacrificed in the process, and a number of structures of dubious design put up in their place.

Lancashire Evening Telegraph

Above: Darwen's Market House and Municipal Buildings in a scene from the 1950s. The rooftops of the market area can be seen in foreground and several period motor vehicles are parked without restriction in the centre of the picture. Talking of restrictions, motorists were now able to buy petrol without coupons as petrol rationing had ended in May 1950. By 1958 yellow 'No Waiting' lines began to appear on the streets of our towns for the first time, much to the annoyance of motorists and some shopkeepers who predicted a decline in trade as a consequence.

Top: 'Buy Your Daily Mail Here!' proclaimed the advert above Adamson's tobacconist in this 1960s scene. Adamsons had been established at least a century and a half before this picture was taken. The focus of this picture is the busy corner of Church street and King William Street, and many famous names from the world of retailing are shown. One which is not as much famous, but still very memorable, is the jewellers which went under the name of Sagar, shown on the right of *Adamsons*. Countless courting couples stood with their noses pressed against the plate glass choosing the engagement rings which would mark the start of their lives together. Gloves for the wedding could be found at *The Glove Shop* around the corner, and matching shoes supplied by Stead and Simpsons. The proud groom would often be kitted out by *Burtons*. If finance was a problem (and when wasn't it?) you could always have a word with the manager of Lloyds Bank next door.

A rooftop view of Darwen looking towards the Market House and the Municipal Buildings. The scene is thought to date from the late 1950s. Darwen was incorporated as a borough in 1878 when the population in the town was approximately 25,000 in number. This view shows the normally busy market area and the adjacent bus lanes from which tired shoppers would take the service home after a trip to the town centre.

Above: There have been many changes to the area known as *Salford* since this picture was taken in 1958. The shops in Church Street are in view, but the location was dominated by the huge modern F. W. Woolworth store. The entrance to the underground lavatories can be seen with the sturdy but ornate iron railings forming a guard at the surface. Beyond them are the public phone boxes and the newsagents shop sporting a large Daily Dispatch advert to attract customers along this busy thoroughfare. In the foreground is the roundabout complete with traffic light apparently 'growing' out of the carefully tended beds. The 'Keep Left' signs which served to remind drivers of the correct direction in which to travel around the traffic islands are neatly recessed in the wall of the obstacle. Subtle evidence of the pride which was taken in the appearance of Blackburn's so-called 'street furniture' at the time.

Top: An elevated view of the *new Daily Market* taken in the mid 1960s from the roof of Dutton's Brewery and featuring the roof-top car park which had been incorporated into the building. The Royal Cinema was still standing when this picture was taken. Extensive use of glass and modern materials gave the structure an extremely progressive look, ably captured by the photograph in a way not so easily seen from the ground. The Yin Kin Chinese restaurant is featured too. Diners would travel from all over Lancashire to sample the delights of this highly reputed eating house, long before the time when every street corner had either a Chinese, Italian or American restaurant located upon it.

Above: The late 1950s was the background against which this scene was set. The corner of Victoria Street and Ainsworth Street was the location of the Blackburn street scene which also features the Golden Lion Hotel. The ornate facade of the *Golden Lion Vaults* is visible on the left of the picture, on Ainsworth Street. Readers may remember trips to some of the small retail establishments shown on the right of the scene. These include Isaac Talbot, noted for his fresh English and continental fruit produce, Whalley's the tobacconists and Hilton's the boot and shoe retailer. Back in 1958 the plucky little Austin A35 van would have been a common sight on the roads in the district. It was derived from the popular A30/ A35 saloon and from a total production run of 576,672 vehicles some 210,000 vans were sold.

A Ribble single decker bus makes its way through Darwen town centre in the mid 1960s. The Midland Bank is featured on the right of the picture in a delightful tudor-style building complete with a stylish turret. Readers may remember the Nan Fung Chinese restaurant further along the street. These were the days long before every street corner had a pizza or hamburger restaurant, though Wimpey Bars were well established by this time. Chinese and Indian restaurants were relatively few and far between and still considered exotic by most ordinary folk. Tramway Furnishers sold good quality, affordable furnishings from their shop next to the restaurant and the railings along this section of busy pavement served to protect shoppers from the cars on the busy main road.

These two local buses look as if they had paused for a 'chat' on a quiet town centre street in the 1960s. Buses had completely taken over from Blackburn's trams from 1949. At their peak the tramway system had carried up to 50,000 people per day on the routes around Blackburn. Lloyds Bank can be seen on the left of the picture and a popular Thwaites house is featured further along the street.

Bird's eye view

A little detective work was required in order to work out the likely date when this picture was taken. The Boulevard can be seen at the bottom of the picture and use of a magnifying glass enabled us to see the distinctive outline of a double deck tramcar. As the last Blackburn tram ran in 1949 the picture must have been taken before that time. Just above the Boulevards Blackburn Cathedral can be seen with half completed extensions on the right hand side of it. The diocese of St. Mary's was created in 1927 and plans were set in place to upgrade the Parish Church to Cathedral status. Funds were raised and building work began in 1938. The outbreak of war in 1939 interrupted the building work and it was not restarted until about 1951. Our best guess is that this picture was taken sometime after the end of the war and the end of the tramway era in 1949. Several other interesting buildings are featured in this view including St. George's Hall along Northgate, the old Town Hall, stained with years of exposure to sooty deposits. The old clock tower near the market area is in view and a good impression of the tightly-packed streets of terraced housing is given. This was the *Blackburn* we knew before the dawn of the massive changes which altered the face of the town just a few years after this picture was taken the new inner relief road system and shopping and civic centres would soon change her face forever.

Left: This picture dates from the first years of the 1960s and shows the development of the centre of the town with work on the development in front of the old Town Hall well under way. The Cathedral extensions are clearly in view near the new bus station, and the whole of the foreground is dominated by the railway lines criss-crossing their way into Blackburn's railway station. On the right of the picture Thwaites Brewery with its distinctive roof can just be seen. There seems still to be a grimy appearance to most of the buildings in the picture, and no wonder. In the early 1960s it was still too soon to see the benefit of the Clean Air Act on the walls of our public buildings. Residents in northern towns would have to wait another decade or so before their towns received the clean-up campaigns they had longed for.

Below left: Taken in the 1920s, this early aerial view was taken looking towards Blackburn from a propeller-driven aircraft flying at 2000 feet. In the foreground an open field is being worked by a farmer and his horse, in the shadow of the expanding Whitbirk Power Station. The busy railway line can be seen running diagonally across the top right hand corner of the photograph.

It runs across and above the arterial road and the canal. It is interesting, though not especially surprising, to see the forest of erect chimneys cluttering the skyline. They were responsible for much of the pollution in the town, along with thousands of domestic fires which combined to pose a danger to public health. The 1955 Clean Air Act compelled local councils to restrict the airborne pollution caused by burning coal, but it would take many years before ordinary people felt the benefits.

Below: An aerial view of *Blackburn Generating Station* taken from an altitude of 2000 feet during September 1948. The third cooling tower can be seen with scaffolding around the top of it, confirming that it is still under construction. The cooling towers were demolished in May 1982. When this picture was taken Britain was going through a period of nationalisation. The electricity industry itself was taken into public ownership in April 1948, just four months after the creation of British Railways. Two years before, in February 1946, the Bank of England had been nationalised and one of Britain's finest achievements, the creation of the National Health Service, took place in November the same year.

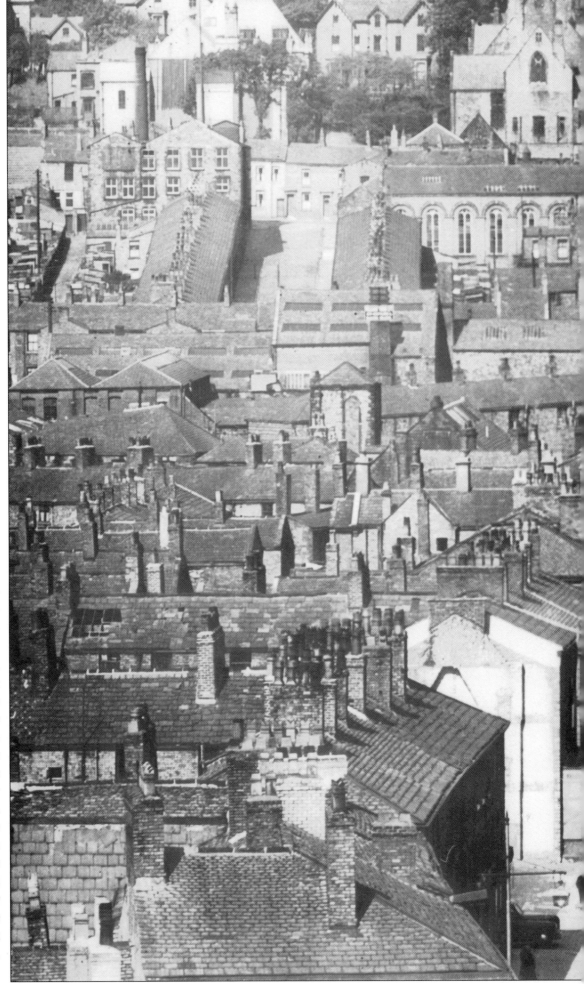

The Montague Street area as it appeared during the late 1940s or early 1950s. Scores of tall domestic chimneys can be seen, but no television aerials let alone satellite dishes at this time of course. Trinity Methodist Church is in the picture and there seem to be far more pedestrians and fewer motor vehicles than we might see in a modern scene.

Sporting life

Below: *Proud members of the Blackburn Rovers team pose for a picture during the 1954/5 season, complete with mascot looking as pleased as Punch to be sat with his heroes. Left to right the players are (back row) Ronnie Clayton, Ron Suart, Tommy Briggs, Reg Elvy, Eric Bell and Willie Kelly. Seated at the front are: Frank Mooney, Eddie Crossan, Bill Eckersley, Eddie Quigley and Bobby Langton. During this season 'Rovers ended sixth in Division Two and were knocked out in the first round of the F.A.Cup by Swansea in front of a crowd of 34,337. The highlight of the season was a 9-0 win against Middlesbrough in November at Ewood Park before a crowd of just over 29,000. The season had got off to a poor start with a 5-1 defeat by Fulham on August 28th.*

Bottom: *Bryan Douglas in action in front of a full-house at Ewood Park. Douglas was born within a stones' throw of the Blackburn ground and he made the first of 438 League appearances for the club in 1954. One of the most popular right wingers the club has ever had, he scored 101 goals for Blackburn Rovers in the League and 11 others in various Cup competitions. In 1953 Bryan Douglas made his first appearance for his country in the England Under 23 team, and the following year he played for the England senior team against Wales. By June 1963 he had made the last of his 36 appearances for England and in 1969 he played his last game for Blackburn Rovers.*

A thrilling match saw Rovers defeated by Bristol City by six goals to four in October 1955 in front of a crowd of 24,695. Blackburn's goals were scored by Briggs (2), Langton, and Crossan. The season was reasonably successful for the club and they finished 4th from the top of Division Two. In the the F.A. Cup a defeat by West Ham by 3 goals to 2 saw them knocked out in the third round. This picture shows Tommy Burden leaping skyward to head towards goal watched by fellow players Bill Smith, Eric Binns and Ronnie Clayton.

Looking very smart in their suits and overcoats, these Blackburn Rovers players pose for the camera before setting off on the long journey to Cardiff for a tough F.A. Cup tie against the Welsh club in February 1958. Left to right we see Mick McGrath, Bill Smith, Peter Dobing, Harry Leyland, Aly MacLeod, Ron Cairns, Ken Taylor, Roy Vernon, Matt Woods, Ron Clayton, Jock Weddle (Trainer) Roy Stephenson, Bill Eckersley and Bryan Douglas. The Cardiff tie had first been played at Ewood Park watched by a crowd of 45,078

and ending in a 0 - 0 draw. The players are seen setting off to Cardiff for the replay. The team went on to win the match by 2 goals to 1, going through to meet Liverpool in the next round. The Liverpool match was seen by 51,000 fans at home and Rovers won 2 - 1 thanks to goals from Clayton and MacLeod. The cup run was to end with defeat in the semi-finals by Bolton Wanderers with a 2 - 1 scoreline in a match played at Maine Road. The spectacle was witnessed by a crowd of 74,800!

Above: Team talk, 1950s style. The picture dates from January 1959 and features ten players watching trainer Jock Weddle demonstrating how to hold a dirty football without getting mud on your blazer. Weddle was a respected player - he had made 42 League appearances for the club since he was poached from Portsmouth by Bob Crompton in 1938. Together with Jock Wightman he formed a formidable coaching team. Featured here are: (back row, left to right): Bill Smith, Roy Isherwood, Harry Leyland, Dave Whelan, Bob Jones, Bill Eckersley and Roy Stephenson. Front Row: Jock Weddle, Matt Woods, Ron Clayton, Ken and Taylor.

Below: An action-packed scene from 'Rovers first game of the 1959-60 season on August 22nd. This was the season which saw Rovers reach the F.A. Cup Final at Wembley after beating Sunderland, Blackpool, Spurs, Burnley and Sheffield Wednesday. The Final, against Wolverhampton Wanderers, was seen by 100,000 fans, many of whom had travelled down from the North. Sadly Rovers lost by 3 goals to nil.

The Darwen End of Ewood Park await the start of the cup match against Liverpool on March 1 1958. The match was seen by a crowd of 51,000. Blackburn had already beaten Rotherham United (4 - 1 away), Everton (2 - 1 away watched by 75, 818), and Cardiff City. Notice the bulky wooden rattles carried by many of the fans in this picture and the bank of enormous loudspeakers for the P.A. system hanging on the edge of the stand roof.

Right: Queues wait patiently for the chance to buy a ticket for the Semi Final match with Sheffield Wednesday. The clash took place at Maine Road Manchester on 26th March, attended by a crowd of 74,135. Two goals from Derek Dougan gave Blackburn victory and a place in the next round. This young policeman was left holding the baby when the photographer captured the scene outside the ground.

Below: Sunday March 13th 1960, and eager fans queue for tickets for the replay of the derby cup match against Burnley. The day before this scene was recorded Blackburn had drawn 3 - 3 at Burnley in a thrilling end-to-end game, and the replay was set for March 16th at Ewood Park. The queue looks orderly enough in this scene, with little to do for the handful of police officers detailed to attend. There must have been at least an element of frustration among the waiting fans, there being only one small window from which tickets were being sold. No doubt any complaint would be met by the response "I've only got one pair of hands you know!" As it turned out, the tickets proved well worth waiting for, and fans saw Rovers beat the lads from Burnley by two goals to nil at the replay. The Cup Final which eventually followed on May 7th saw Blackburn Rovers loose to Wolverhampton Wanderers with a 3 - 0 scoreline.

Below: Corner shops have been a feature of northern life for longer than anyone can remember. Their popularity has come and gone over the years in response to various trends, most of which have been connected with the shopping public's inability to buy anything located more than six feet away from their car boot. Haworth's was a family grocer of the traditional kind which could be found here at Nab Lane. This is an early 1960s photograph, two major clues as to the approximate date being the Austin Cambridge (remembered for the startled look it seemed to have on its 'face') and the television aerial standing some eight or ten feet above the rooftops. Television ownership began to take off with the coverage of the 1953 Coronation, and gathered momentum as important football matches and national events such as Churchill's funeral were televised.

Bottom: The Palatine Dairies stall supplied keenly-priced butter, cream, milk (of all types) and even Horlicks. The integral milk bar was a popular oasis for weary housewives and the occasional offspring to recharge their batteries in the middle of a busy shopping spree. Two of the ladies featured here look less than pleased at the prospect of having their picture taken. Perhaps they were concerned at the thought of their 10 minutes of relaxation appearing for all to see in the local paper? They would never have guessed that we would still be talking about them around fifty years later!

Shopping spree

Certain to bring back memories of trips to the indoor market, this picture was taken in November 1952. Some of the better known stalls are featured, including A. Holliday and Sons, Joe Littler and the Palatine Dairies and Cafe. Munroe's can just be seen in the distance. Our eye was draw to the expression on the face of the little lad just left of centre. His attention had been caught by a display on the counter of Joe Littler's stall featuring a whole pig glaring out at the passing customers. The boy looks rather unsure about what to make of the exhibit - and no wonder. This is the stuff nightmares are made of!

Piles of fruit and vegetable boxes litter the pavement as two elderly ladies pick their way through the obstacles in the Market Place. The open market area located in this part of Blackburn had been laid out in the latter part of the nineteenth century. This picture dates from the early 1960s. A popular high street bank can be seen in the distance, and the camera is pointed in the direction of New Market Street.

Lancashire Evening Telegraph

Above: It didn't begin to rival Blackpool Illuminations, but these Thwaites Arcade Christmas lights were a welcome and worthwhile attempt at getting shoppers into the Christmas spirit. The Thwaites Arcade was built in 1883 and had connections with the family of local brewers which shared the same name. The arcade formed an interesting link between Lord Street and Church Street. Tears were shed by some local people when it was listed for demolition in the redevelopment of the 1970s. It was finally pulled down in 1971.
Left: An unusual rooftop view of the interior of the indoor market which dates from 1963. The distinctive iron pillars will be familiar to many readers. All the stalls had a very similar frontage, strictly controlled by the markets management to ensure uniformity. The sights and sounds of the market area (not to mention the distinctive aromas found there) created indelible memories in the minds of the people who visited it. Market trading has been a feature of life in Blackburn for many centuries, and the quality an value of the goods on offer has attracted people into the town from many miles around.

Right: *A trip to the shops or the market, as seen here, required three essential components in the 1960s: A hat (or a headscarf), an ankle-length overcoat and a shopping bag large enough to carry three months' supplies of groceries in the event of the outbreak of a world war or unexpected Bank Holiday. The winter months required additional clothing, usually taking the form of black fur-lined booties to protect the ankles and a transparent plastic rainhood to protect the latest shampoo and set. Shopping was more than a chore, it was a social pursuit with its own rituals and routines, conducted at a time when life was enjoyed at a slower pace than it does today, a time when people seemed to have time for a friendly word or two in the course of their dealings with each other.*

Below: *This view is certain to bring back memories of shopping at the old enclosed and open markets. A sea of canvass covers the tops of the stalls, protecting the fresh produce and the market traders from the heat of the sun. On damp days the canvass kept the rainwater away and allowed trade to continue unrestricted. There was something symbolic about the market clock tower and most Blackburn folk felt deep affection for it. There was sadness when it was swept away to make room for modern shops and the Civic offices as part of Blackburn's modernisation programme. The Austin 1100 saloon on the left was able to park here without much trouble. The ground-breaking design incorporated many features found in the Mini, including the transverse engine and 'hydrolastic' suspension for which it was well-known. With four doors, lively performance and good fuel economy it soon became a winner with the motoring public.*

Lancashire Evening Telegraph

Below: This picture dates from 1927 and the station clock suggests the time was 1.45 p.m. It features a variety of transport networks as they converge on Blackburn's unique (for the time) Boulevard transport interchange. Here the rival methods of transport would come together and passengers would either make their way to their destination on foot or switch to one of the other networks. Buses, trains and trams formed the basis of their options - car ownership at this time was growing but still limited to the wealthiest families. The proximity of the Boulevard to the centre of Blackburn was a boon for shoppers and retailers, as well as the people concerned with industry and commerce in the town. The growth of the public transport system made it possible for people live further away from their place of work and, as a consequence, for the development of suburban communities. This pattern was repeated in towns and cities throughout the country.

Above: An almost desolate scene at Brownhill Roundabout which dates from 1935. Road signs mark the route to Burnley and Clitheroe in the distance, but sadly any trace of the traffic they were intended to direct is absent from the scene. A gas lamp on the left of the picture reminds us of the era from which the photograph dates. In modern times this might be a highly prized feature of a posh suburban garden. But isn't it strange how modern *reproduction* gas lamps never quite capture the perfect proportions of the originals? The tram lines on the main road remind us of the importance of that particular form of public transport, as does the tram shelter on the other side of the road. Keen eyes may just be able to make out the mess left by another form of transport. Horse power was not as environmentally-friendly as some would have us think!

The staff at Blackburn's busy railway station had a well-earned reputation for throwing their weight behind local celebrations and events of many kinds. The busy station hall was an ideal place to promote events to the thousands of people who passed through it each week. The 1951 centenary celebrations were a good excuse to get the banners out as this picture shows. The spindly hand carts and trailers used for transferring all kinds of packages between trains and waiting road

transport add character to the scene. These were the days when everything from milk to newspapers were transporting by rail - the days before Britain's motorway network was established and Doctor Beeching axed much of the railway's resources. Note the cheeky sign advertising the Burnley Building Society on the station wall and the posters offering return tickets to Morecambe for just 3/9 - less than 20p in modern currency.

Right: A return ticket to Blackpool could be yours for just 3s 3d (about 17p) when this picture was taken in the 1950s. This was the offer displayed on a poster outside the L.M.S Railway Station. It was 5.10 p.m according to the clock on the station roof and people can be seen making their way home from this busy transit point. Precariously positioned crates can be seen on the light-coloured Dutton's wagon in the centre of the picture, itself surrounded by double decker buses arriving to collect the workers and shoppers making their way home.

Below: This magnificent float was constructed by the Lion Brewery as part of Blackburn's Centenary celebrations. The vehicle was limited to speeds of 20 m.p.h when performing its usual task of making deliveries to Blackburn's licensed premises, but even this slow pace might have been a bit on the risky side for the precariously placed bottles and barrels shown here. The picture dates from 1951.

A very crowded scene at Blackburn's Boulevard which dates from the 1950s. Several memorable buildings can be seen in the background, including the Adelphi Hotel and the roof of *Duttons* beyond it. The Pearl Assurance offices are just about in the centre of the picture, in the distance, and moving across to the right we see the premises of Sydney Smith the taxi proprietor and funeral director. You would be showing your age if you admitted to knowing that *Glendower Tea Tips* were renowned for their fine flavour - the company had invested heavily in advertisements on the sides of many of these buses. Tea was big business in the 1950s.

Below: This 1950s scene will bring back memories among those who used the Boulevard transport interchange at the time. The very utilitarian style of the bus was typical of the vehicles which took over from the tramcars which had provided sterling service for half a century. Redundant tram lines can still be seen in this picture, striking a hard edge along the smoothly rounded cobbles.

Right: Conditions may have been grim on ocassions but there was usually time for a warm smile and friendly chat in the street communities around Blackburn. These were the days when people routinely left their doors unlocked - or open, without fear of someone running off with their television. Of course, they didn't *have* a television, but you know what we mean! These days the neighbourly culture which we used to take for granted has disappeared from many areas and some people seem to know the characters in the popular soap operas better than the people next door. It would be unusual, to say the least, to see a modern housewife scrubbing the pavement outside her house in the 1990s!

On the home front

Lancashire Evening Telegraph

The rather clinical wording on the back of this print reads 'a typical fire range of an operative's cottage in Lund Street.' Clearly there is a lot more to this scene than those words suggest. For a start, the photograph was taken much more recently than people may think; readers may be surprised to learn that it dates from only 1963, the year which saw the assassination of President Kennedy, the first kidney transplant (at a Leeds hospital), and the Great Train Robbery. News of some of these events might have occupied the mind of this old gentleman as he rocks in his chair and stares at the glowing embers of his fire. The range played several important roles in the home. When meticulously black-leaded to a mirror finish it represented a symbol of pride. In more practical terms it provided heat and a place for cooking, baking and washing. It was here that the iron would be heated prior to pressing and ironing the weekly wash, which, as can be seen here, was frequently dried above the range. All this makes us wonder 'how do we manage without a range in our homes today?'

At work

Left: This almost artistic scene shows a little lad and his granny making their way along a back street of Blackburn in the 1960s. Rows of terraced houses characterised much of the streets in the centre of town, they had been hastily constructed for the most part to house the thousands of workers who toiled in the local mills. Built in the days before an effective public transport system existed, it was important that the houses were within walking distance of the places of employment. Typically, the houses had only the most basic of facilities. Even supplies of running water (save that from the damp walls) could not be taken for granted. Some relied upon communal outside lavatories at the end of the street. These would become dirty and were frequently vandalised; the individual outside toilets attached to other houses were considered a great improvement. Bathrooms were only as common as swimming pools are today in some districts, and residents relied upon their galvanised tin baths to stay clean.

Above: Some of the building work which characterised the redevelopment which took place in Blackburn during the 1960s. The work shown here was officially known as the 'Town Centre Redevelopment Phase 1' by the people responsible for it. There is a stark contrast between the traditional styling of the old Town Hall in the background and the spiky concrete foundations being laid by the workmen for the modern development. The original Town Hall was designed James Paterson and built by Richard Hacking and William Stones. Opening in 1856 the building served as Blackburn's Court, the location of the local Police Headquarters (complete with cells), the home of the Chief Constable and the official seat of local government.

A group of old fire engines was polished and parked-up outside the old fire station for this historic photograph which was taken in the 1940s. The long ladders seen on two of the appliances were essential items of equipment, particularly when tackling the all-too-frequent blazes at local mills. Mills were particularly prone to the devastating fires we remember from our childhood. Oil-soaked timbers, dry, flammable textile material and dubious electrical wiring combined to create the conditions that firemen hate. Blackburn owes much to the bravery of generations of professional firefighters whose vigilance and skill have been assets the town.

Lancashire Evening Telegraph

Above: The demands of modern shopping and the need to relieve the centre of Blackburn of the choking congestion caused by slow moving road transport, caused the redevelopment of the town centre in the 1960s. During the transformation that took place the whole of the central shopping area endured disruption as the controversial glass and concrete structures replaced the familiar old buildings which had formerly occupied the same land. The old market and much-loved clock tower (which stood on the site now occupied by the modern shopping precinct and the tower block extension to the Town Hall) was cleared. The area for the bright new market building employing the latest design and construction techniques sat between Ainsworth Street and Penney Street, Salford. Blackburn was one of the first major towns in the North West to undergo such a 'root and branch' reorganisation of its central shopping area and the changes took the best part of 20 years to complete.

The aircraft that won the war

During the planning of the expansion of the aircraft industry steps were taken to guard against enemy attack on factories by placing new ones away from the vulnerable areas of South East England and the Midlands. The development of the English Electric factories complied with this principle as NW England was considered to be a relatively safe area.

The extent to which production of large aircraft could be scattered was limited because particularly large buildings were required. The main effort was therefore directed towards having single parts and small assemblies made in smaller premises in the region of the main factory. The English Electric Strand Road, East Works factory in Preston was intended to build large heavy bombers so that there was no reasonable possibility of dispersing the bulk of production work. Large scale dispersion was not considered particularly necessary in the NW of

England. Nearby factories were requisitioned, including part of premises owned by Courtaulds, Austin House, a motor agent's premises and Stephenson's Foundry.

Above: Installing the engine on a Halifax Bomber at Samlesbury. *Below:* English Electric bomber assembly in No. 4 shed at Samlesbury.

After the war, it was discovered that the Luftwaffe did undertake aerial reconnaissance of the area. Photographs from August 29th 1940 show the boundaries of the English Electric factory had been accurately marked by German aerial intelligence. With the photographs was an analysis of the buildings of the factory, accurately interpreting the type and area of each building. However, the factory was identified as an 'Electrical Machine Works' and German intelligence seems to have been unaware that aircraft work had been in progress there for more than two years.

By April 1939 the only part of the expansion programme not yet implemented was the flight test aerodrome. The site selected was at Samlesbury, six miles east of the Preston factory. The land had been earmarked for a civil airport to serve Preston and Blackburn, but had not been developed. It was situated on rising, open country, midway between Preston and Blackburn since labour could be recruited from both towns.

Construction of the first hangar was started on 10th April 1939 and completed in October of that year. This was the only hangar available for final assembly of the early-production Hampdens. The construction of two tarmac runways had begun in August.

As Hampden production was gathering momentum, English Electric received instructions from the Air Ministry to prepare for the production of 100 Halifax heavy bombers. The Halifax was at this time in the very early stages of development at Handley Page and the prototype was not to fly for another eight months. The first contract for Halifaxes was received in April 1940 and called for 200 aircraft.

Steady progress was meanwhile made towards the initial flight of the first Hampden and steps were taken to increase production capacity at Strand Road. The West Works there was taken over to provide capacity for the expected

Above: Canberra aircraft under assembly in No. 4 Shed.
Facing page bottom: A Halifax Mk II MZ868 almost complete in No. 2 Shed, Samlesbury in July 1944.
Left: A Handley Page Hampden bomber at Samlesbury early in the war.

orders for Halifax production. Further extensions continued to be made into 1940.

The first hangar at Samlesbury having been opened, work started in May 1940 on a second which was to be several times larger and was intended to be used eventually for Halifax final assembly.

Major assemblies for the first Hampden were transferred from the Strand Road factory to Samlesbury for final assembly on the last day of 1939.

Soon afterwards the tarmac runways were completed, six weeks before the first aircraft was ready to fly.

The first Hampden flew on 22nd February 1940 and was delivered in March. Only 14 months had elapsed between the contract being received and the first flight. This short period saw the introduction of a relatively complex aircraft into the Preston factory, followed by modification and extension of the work itself, the building of the flight test aerodrome and a six fold increase in employees.

In August, plans for two more hangars at Samlesbury were approved, to be used initially for Hampden repair and modification work. Both were completed in the second half of 1941, as were the runway extensions. The last and largest hangar on the site was completed in December 1942, after which construction was started on a concrete

runway which was finished in May 1943.

At the end of the war Strand Road and Samlesbury could both report no damage by enemy action and no aircraft had been lost before it had been passed to the customer.

Considering the large number built this record is particularly creditable. The only significant accident was when a Halifax, flown

by an RAF pilot, burst a tyre on landing and was seriously damaged after leaving the runway and colliding with a large concrete mixer. Wartime production had not sacrificed quality for quantity, the safety record during flight testing being an important indication of this fact.

By the end of the war the cut back of orders resulted in Halifax production at Preston being terminated after 2,500 had been delivered and Vampire orders being reduced. Only six Vampires had been completed by the end of the fighting but the type was one of those chosen to re-equip the post war RAF and it therefore remained in production.

Even so, much of the factory capacity was available for non-aircraft work. Manufacture of diesel and electric locomotives, railway rolling stock and electric motors was recommenced, these items having been the prewar products of the factory buildings, along with trams.

The Vampire work that remained at Preston served a valuable purpose. Continuity of aircraft production experience was maintained in the period when English Electric had no aircraft of its own design ready for manufacture.

Above: De Havilland Vampires at Samlesbury.
Left: VIPs visit the Halifax Assembley Shed.

Geo. Broughton & Co - oiling the wheels of industry in Lancashire

Geo Broughton & Co is a family business with a history that spans almost 80 years. Beginning life as East Lancashire Lubricants, it was founded by George Broughton and his business partner at the time, J. Bentley.

George was a forward thinking man who realised that lubricating oil was something that the increasingly mechanised world could not live without. At that time motor cars were still a rarity on the roads but were still a rarity on the roads but were just beginning to make their presence felt.

It was this that persuaded George to resign from his office job at Imperial Mill, where his father was secretary and strike out with J. Bentley in Cook Street, blending and supplying the lubricants needed to keep the wheels turning. The street, which was situated off Copy Nook no longer exists.

These were the tenuous foundations for the company which today handles millions of litres of oil, distributing fuels and lubricants from major oil companies, including Castrol, to a wide variety of industries.

Some time in the 1920s Bentley moved on, leaving George as

Above: George Broughton, founder of the company. *Centre: A 1964 advert for Gebrol's Heating Oils.* *Right: The company's first brand new tanker, a Bedford TK.*

sole owner. He changed the name to Geo. Broughton & Co. By 1928 the business had expanded to such an extent that it required new premises. A move was made to Whitebirk Road, into a building that had once housed the horses belonging to Whitebirk Colliery and later the offices of a local brickworks. The company still trades from these works today.

The Second World War curbed trade because oil supplies were commandeered for the war effort. It was a difficult time for the company, as it was for most but in 1942 it became a limited liability company.

In 1948, George was joined in the company by his son Rex, who had recently been de-mobbed from the Royal Navy. Over the next ten years the use of lubri-

You're assured of a
WARM RECEPTION

Gebrol
Heating
Oils

FOR THE

NEW
STARLIGHT
CLUB

SUPPLIED BY

GEO. BROUGHTON
AND COMPANY LTD.

WHITEBIRK, BLACKBURN
Tel.: 53644
★ 24 Hours Fuel Oil Delivery Service ★

decline as heating oil escalated in price. At this awkward time the third generation of the family became involved in the business, with Rex's son, Ian, joining in 1978. He had previously worked as a research chemist for a major oil company in the field of lubricating oils and greases.

During the 1980s the business went full circle as Ian went back into the supply of lubricants, this time the more specialised end of the market. Today the firm supplies oils for most industries and has years of technical expertise, which gives it the edge over the competition, an expertise which is unique amongst small oil distributors.

cants for machinery in the cotton mills started to decline and in the late 1950s Rex made the decision to diversify into the supply of fuel oils. A five gallon home delivery service was started.

The very first delivery of tractor vaporising oil caused the company a few headaches. The farmer who placed the order wanted a staggering 280 gallons and the company had to supply it in five-gallon drums. The load filled both of Broughton's small vans. Such orders were tying up the vans for a whole day and it was decided to buy an Austin three-way load van, which was equipped with a 300 gallon tank and a hand pump. Eventually in 1960 the firm bought its first bulk tanker, a Morris Commercial, from National Benzol for £325. Shortly after the brand name Gebrol was introduced, devised by Rex, as a shortened version of the full company name.

The 1960s saw rapid growth in the use of oil fired central heating and the company soon had a fleet of tankers supplying homes, farms and industry with paraffin and heating oils. The two oil price shocks in 1974 and 1979 sent this market into temporary

Ian is now managing director and Rex has retired although he still retains a keen interest in transport and tankers. Company growth is slow but steady in this very competitive market, the firm has at least two competitors in Blackburn itself, as well as some in the surrounding towns. There is, however, hope for the future with a fourth generation of the family waiting in the wings and if this new generation is as successful as its predecessors then the future of the company is bright.

Top: The company's very first tanker, a Morris Commercial, bought in 1960. Above: The premises in the late 1960s. Left: Part of today's fleet.

Cobble - leading the world in tufting machinery technology

Like many other industries, tufting began as a cottage industry in the USA, manufacturing candlewick bedspreads either by hand, or on converted domestic sewing machines. At the time, cotton, which grew abundantly in the area was the main pile material.

The Cobble brothers, Bud and Jake, began their business in the Calhoun Chattanooga, Tennessee area of America in 1936. Both men were engineers and worked as a team to mechanise the tufting process.

The first 50" wide machine was made in 1940 by the Cobble Brothers and was still used for candlewick bedspreads. World War II curtailed any further advances. In 1946 the Cobble Brothers resumed the venture and made a candlewick machine 115" wide, in 5/8" gauge.

Three years later they were producing 9'and 12' carpet tufting machines, using cotton as the main pile material.

The business developed in Tennessee before expanding into post war Europe. The United kingdom was chosen because of the obvious advantage of having no language barriers. There was also the added bonus of providing jobs for recession hit Britain, including construction opportunities.

1953 saw the birth of the UK Tufting Industry in Blackburn with the formation of Tufting Machinery Limited, which later became 'BTM' - British Tufting Machinery Limited. Their first machines were 3/16" and 5/32" in gauge and 5, 9 and 12' in width.

Above: A lock stitching machine in the late 1950s.
Left: A front view of a Controlled Needle machine, showing the Pattern Drum. The picture dates from the 1960s.

Cobble purchased the share capital of BTM in 1961, and was soon to be taken over by Singer USA - hence Singer-Cobble was born.

In the same year, Ellison Tufting Machinery was formed by ex-employees of Cobble and BTM. Both they, and Singer-Cobble began to manufacture finer gauges than the original 3/16", 1/8" and 5/32" - thus enabling the UK tufting industry to make a big step forward.

In 1955 the Cobble Brothers set up a subsidiary company in what is now Cobble Blackburn Ltd., Gate Street, Blackburn, at first importing American made machines and later, manufacturing units to the American design. At this time, BTM started to manufacture other carpet related equipment such as backing and drying plant, creels and carpet cutting machinery.

By 1956, Blackburn had two well established tufting machinery manufacturers, who successfully managed to introduce tufting to the rest of Europe and both the Middle and Far East.

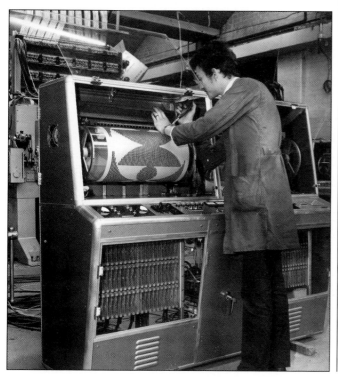

On the Continent, attitudes towards tufting were also changing - by the mid 1960s the tufting industry was flourishing across Europe.

1964 saw the arrival of the Edgar Pickering Company and in 1966 two more tufting machinery manufacturers emerged - Universal Tufting Machinery and Pendhill Engineering. The companies worked side by side, many of its employees knowing each other well.

On one occasion in the 1960s, a Cobble employee was at Capetown Airport in South Africa, waiting for his flight home when he bumped into a Cobble Pickering colleague who was booked onto a later flight. After some negotiation with the airport authorities they agreed to his request to return home with his colleague on the later flight. Whilst they were still waiting for their flight in the lounge, enjoying a drink together, an announcement was made over the tannoy that the flight that the Cobble employee was originally booked onto had crashed, twenty minutes into its journey, killing all on board.

Above: Mrs Spedding, wife of the then Singer Cobble managing director, Bob Spedding (sixth from the left) cutting the ground at the site of the new Singer Cobble factory at Haslingden Road, circa 1970.
Left: A remote controlled pattern drum in the 1970s.

Remarkably, considering the number of flight hours undertaken by Cobble employees, this was the nearest that any have come to a aircraft disaster.

In spite of the proliferation of tufting machine manufacturers by the mid 1960s the United Kingdom still produced more woven than tufted carpet. However in 1967 the situation changed, and for the first time, tufting production increased and overtook that of woven carpets.

Between 1966 and 1974, the tufting machinery industry continued to develop and expand, allowing Singer-Cobble and Pickering to dominate the market. Tufting machinery production peaked In 1973/74 - more than 20 machines were dispatched from

Blackburn based companies per month.

Gauges as fine as 1/20" were developed commercially and tufting penetrated

the UK market, accounting for in excess of 65% of total carpet production.

In 1973, the Pickering Company was sold to Sears Holdings. The decline in the market, post 1974, precipitated the inevitable reorganisation of the industry - companies such as Ellison, Universal and Pendhill ceased machinery manufacture.

In 1977, Spencer Wright Industries bought the Cobble Group from Singer. In 1980, the Cobble Group of Spencer Wright Industries bought the Pickering companies from Sears Holdings. In the 1980s, the industry experienced a modest recovery.

Sixty years on, tufting has developed from the basic principles into a highly sophisticated

computer controlled business. Cobble technicians and engineers utilise advanced technology to produce the world's finest, fastest, most accurate and reliable tufting machinery. Approximately 90% of Cobble's business is for export markets. Today Cobble dominate these markets supplying more than 80% of tufting machines outside of America, exporting to over 40 countries worldwide, including Benelux, mainland Europe, the Middle and Far East.

Above: Former Blackburn Labour MP, Barbara Castle with Eric Crossley, a former sales director of Singer Cobble, circa 1977.
Left: An Asquith Drilling Machine.
Below: A modern Cobble ST91 Two Pile height full repeat scroll tufting machine.

Sandersons confectioners - from mining to dining

The initiative of a retired Blackburn miner and his wife in 1949 led to the flourishing business everyone recognises in Blackburn today as the source of Sandersons' pies!

Having left the pit and equipped themselves with one small upright mixer, one small, two-deck coke oven and about six bags of flour, John and Alice Sanderson, with the help of their son Clarence, set up a small cafe and bakery at Mellor Brook, Blackburn. Clarence was the baker, Alice looked after the cafe.

In the early 1970s, Clarence was joined by his brother, Cyril and later that decade by his two sons, Glyn and Martin. By 1984 the business had grown so that more space was needed. In spite of some unfriendly government legislation and no question of grants, there was a further expansion. A new bakery was opened, Ramsgreave Bakery, at Pleckgate Road, the site which had once housed Haydock's Laundry.

It was vandalised to the point of ruin and it took twelve months' hard graft to get the property how they wanted it. When it was ready for them to move in, Sandersons decided to retain the Mellor Brook building and continue to run

it as a retail outlet. The new premises became the bakery, this time furnished with the latest equipment, including a bread plant, French stick machines, a ten-rack prover, automatic pie machines, 6-ton flour silos -and the rest! There was also a computerised office manned by three staff.

As well as their own shops, Sandersons now supply to 350 outlets which include shops, schools and hospitals. A fleet of five vans delivers from bakery to customer. Blackburn mouths water as they go by!

Above: The premise in the 1980s.
Top: A pre Second World War picture of the bakery at Mellor Brook.
Left: ...and how they look today.

Tommy Ball - the entrepreneur with the heart of gold

Some thirty five or forty years ago in Blackburn, a rag and bone man named Tommy Ball found that sometimes he was handed shoes that would be quite wearable after a little care and attention. Since shoes were always in demand and were not cheap he began to specialise in repairing and selling second hand shoes.

old textile mill which had to be completely renovated at considerable effort and cost to make it the store it is today.

Helped by Mary, his wife, they took a stall in Blackburn Market which they ran for twenty years before moving to Clifton Street. This was the first of several moves around the town until the premises in Hart Street were purchased.

They were large enough to bring the whole concern under one roof but the building was an

In the early days there was a problem over Sunday opening, which until recently was against the law. Tommy Ball had an ingenious scheme to get round the problem. He formed the Tommy Ball Sunday Club with the help of Blackburn Lions.

It was held, of course, in his shop. An entrance fee of one shilling was collected at the door by one of the 'Lions'. All the shillings went to Blackburn Lions' Charities, together with the five hundred pounds that Tommy Ball paid them for every Sunday he remained open for trade. The money went into a kidney dialysis fund which eventually topped twenty five thousand pounds.

Above: *Tommy Ball's reconditioned shop at Lower Eanam.*
Top: *Tommy Ball on his market stall in the 1950s.*
Right: *The effects of the flood in 1986.*

Thousands of pairs of new shoes are on display at all times in the main shop but Tommy Ball remember the old days and has provided a 'Reconditioned Department' just a few hundred yards from the store. Customers are also offered free parking, a seventy seater restaurant and a children's play area.

To keep the crowds pouring in advertising concentrated each week on a different aspect of footwear. One weekend it was ladies' winter boots, another there was a scoop purchase of men's Italian footwear, then sports shoes, followed by men's working footwear. Naturally, all the rest of the range was available as well for the customers who rolled up.

In 1986 a burst watermain completely flooded the bottom floor of the shop damaging a lot of stock. The staff rallied round to sweep out water and dry floors and the store remained open throughout.

Nowadays the shop closes only on Christmas Day and Easter Sunday.

Offering quality footwear at affordable prices, the store attracts custom from all over the north, from people who know that they will always get value for money.

Above: A late 1970s view of the store, the date evident in the style of shoes and boots on offer at the time.
Left: Tommy Ball's as it is today.
Below: The result of the shillings collected at Tommy Ball's Sunday Club. All the proceeds went to the Kidney Dialysis Fund.

Cherry Tree Machine Co Ltd - bearing fruit for well over a century

The Cherry tree Machine Co. Ltd is a company whose roots in Blackburn go back over a century to 1870, which makes it one of the longest established engineering companies in the north of England. Based at Walker Industrial Park and justly proud of their experience, the company's laundry equipment is known throughout the world.

In the early days their products were supplied to such institutions as workhouses, prisons and hospitals and were constructed of timber and cast iron. They were manually operated and were built to combine a washing drum and mangle arrangement that allowed water to be returned back to the washing fluids. The site at Cherry Tree was chosen because of its location close to the Leeds and Liverpool Canal. Raw materials were delivered by barge.

Today, with modern transportation trends differing greatly from those of the last century, the company has moved to prestigious new offices and manufacturing facilities, conveniently adjacent to the M65 motorway at Walker Industrial Park, Blackburn.

Above: The premises as they appeared at the turn of the century.
Below: A dry cleaning machine dating from 1936.

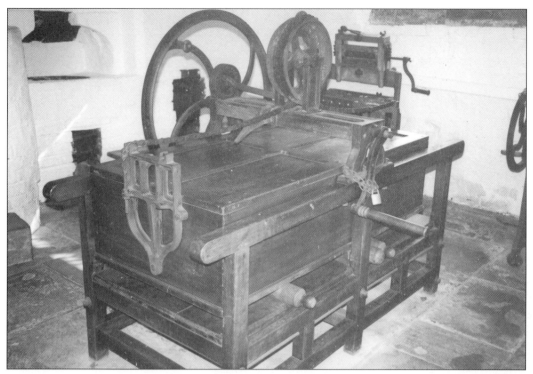

also use the company's machines for dyeing, stonewashing and finishing of garments.

An alliance with G.A. Braun Inc. Syracuse, New York State in 1960 allowed the manufacture of washer extractors to be undertaken in Britain. This saw hundreds of machines being built and supplied to the same market, using the combined expertise of both long-standing companies.

The company places great emphasis on research and technical development, employing a team of mechanical and electronic design engineers who continually up-date product specifications to satisfy ever changing market demands.

Cherry Tree's workforce includes a number of service and installation engineers who are called upon to travel to any part of the world. As the only UK manufacturer of laundry machinery and specialist textile laundry machinery, the company is well placed in the market and has a bright future that is well founded on the experiences of its past.

Above: A box mangle from the early part of the 1900s.
Left: The Cherry Tree Rapid washing machine from 1925.
Below: The company's premises today.

Cherry Tree's market place and customer base has changed dramatically over the years and forced changes in the equipment demanded. Although their machines are still supplied to hospitals and prison laundries, major customers today include commercial laundries involved in workwear rental, hotel laundries and ships. The textile and denim industries

Royal Ordnance - the story of the 'fuze' factory

Royal Ordnance has played a crucial part in the defence of Britain for over 400 years. Since being established as the Royal Powder Mill in 1560 its explosive munitions and weapons have been used from the time of the Spanish Armada to Operation Desert Storm campaigns. The weapons systems produced by Royal Ordnance are in service with the British armed forces and those of many nations worldwide.

Its Blackburn factory, known simply as the Fuze and later as ROF, appeared as war loomed in 1937.

Blackburn was chosen because it was not considered especially vulnerable to air raids and because government ministers had been impressed by the manual dexterity of the ladies at Roe Lee Textile Mill! Work was finished at the present factory at Blackamoor in 1939 though work had begun before that in temporary premises. Only an artist's view of early factory conditions exists because cameras were not allowed. The factory was painted in daubs of brown and green to camouflage

it from above and it was protected by its own Home Guard unit. Further to confuse the enemy, a decoy factory was erected on the moors. Inside the real one, two 12 hour shifts operated seven days a week. There was a proud day in 1941 when King George VI and Queen Elizabeth made a visit. Workers were allowed to see them, then it was straight back to work.

After the important munitions work of the war, tasks like making the insides of alarm clocks seemed a come-down. For a while, though, the factory was grateful to see any work. Soon, however, defence work came in, together with high-tech design manufacturing with civilian applications. Royal Ordnance became a public limited company in 1985 and a wholly owned subsidiary of British Aerospace in 1987.

Many people around Blackburn will notice the demolition of the old Royal Ordnance Factory on Stopes Brow and could be forgiven for believing the activities of Royal Ordnance have ceased in the area.

Above: *A thought-provoking picture dating from 1941, taken by the Luftwaffe. The outline of Royal Ordnance can be seen in the bottom right hand corner.*
Centre left: *men of the 6th Royal West Kent Regiment manning a 3" mortar at Cassino in March 1944.* **Left:** *Fuze test and inspection during the war. Note the tin hats which were for employees use.*

This is most certainly not the case. Though 80% of the site has disappeared for redevelopment and past practices have been abandoned, a new and vibrant business now functions on Roman Road, thanks to the determination and skills of the staff of the new Royal Ordnance Electronics & Fuzes Business.

When spending on defence was reduced in the UK after the ending of the cold war, Royal Ordnance was not idle. It took drastic measures, for example the reduction of its workforce from 2,000 to 380, introduced competitive practices and looked for new markets, trying to decide how the technological skills of the remaining workers could be used for new products.

Above: Machining components during the war years.
Below: King George VI and Queen Elizabeth visited the factory in 1941. Here they are seen with local dignitaries walking around the site.

It was not an easy task. Overseas defence markets are very difficult to penetrate. However, a new portfolio was produced of products that are amongst the best in the world in their niche markets. In fact some of them have become the standard by which competitive products are judged.

The traditional fuze business remains, much pared down and using microchips instead of clockwork. The components business has been sustained, introducing new products to support the other businesses within Royal Ordnance countrywide.

The new company's original speciality was the production of mechanical time fuzes for artillery and anti-aircraft ammunition. It is now a multi-million pound complex with a wide range of military products.

A new simulation business has been developed, enabling troops to fight realistic battles in training and analyse the results without a real shot being fired. Perhaps the most important innovation is the Royal Ordnance Vehicle Intercom System (ROVIS). Military vehicles are notoriously noisy and communications between such vehicles are vital during military action. ROVIS allows their drivers to hear one another whilst gunfire and huge engines are thundering in the background.

Royal Ordnance have over 40 years of experience in producing intercom systems for military application. ROVIS, their latest is now the world standard system. The staff have sufficient faith in it to have produced a demonstration tape which the general public can hear over the telephone.

Royal Ordnance looked for a market to the USA, the biggest users of sophisticated military equipment. Though it has been reduced, US spending power is still huge. To seem like a local supplier, Royal Ordnance selected as a partner a large US company, Northtop Grumman, which makes the B2 Stealth Bomber and set about convincing the customer he needed ROVIS. Today it is the standard intercom for the military market. Through it the business at Blackburn has consolidated and its workforce has risen.

Above: Sailors fitting ROF Blackburn fuzes to 4.5" naval ammunition during the war.
Left: A soldier with a Surface to Air missile, fitted with ROF safety and arming unit during the Falklands War.

Whalleys Hulton & Procter - where the customer always comes first

Way back in 1866 a tinker by the name of Henry Whalley decided to go into business together with his wife as tinsmiths. Premises were taken in Blackburn town centre and the business quietly prospered.

The firm changed hands several times over the years. First it was bought by Arthur Harrison, then later by Rennie and Denis Keighley. Finally it was purchased and taken over by the present owners, Barry Hulton and Stuart Procter.

All of them were sheet metal workers. At the beginning items were manufactured from tinned sheet but now all metals, ferrous and non-ferrous are used in manufacture.

The original premises gave long service. It was seventy five years in fact before it was eventually decided to make a move. The company's new home was in Starkie Street and it stayed here for almost forty years before the final move was made to the present building in Stanley Street.

Business has had its ups and downs. Custom died down during the recessions of the thirties and much later in the eighties. There was an upturn in business during both world wars when the firm was awarded government contracts to contribute to the war effort.

Today Whalleys Hulton & Procter sell mainly to local businesses, local councils and the building trade, in particular to Eric Wright

Construction, Blackburn with Darwen Borough Council, and Lancashire County Council. They supply Graham & Brown, wallpaper specialist, Perseverance Mills (Textiles), Netlon, Acme Refrigeration and Blackburn Technical College.

Whalleys Hulton & Procter continually invest in up-to date technology and wisely always put the customer first. The company is proud to claim that no job is too small and no job is too challenging.

Above: Industrial gates supplied by the company.
Left: An example of ballustrades.
Below: A section wrapping machine for wallpaper, designed and built by the company.

Westholme School: 1923 -1998

On April 18 1923, Miss Emily Singleton opened the doors of her new school in the Trinity Wesleyan Sunday School on Preston New Road. Having close family ties in Blackburn, she wanted to return from Dewsbury where she was teaching to her home town. But this was the time of the Great Depression; there were no jobs to be had. Her friend, Miss Ivy Richmond, was in a similar position. Together they came up with a stunning

solution to their dilemma: if there were no school in a position to take them, then they would have to make their own school. That is precisely what they did and they started with a room in the Sunday School, one cupboard, four folding tables (they had to fold; the whole school was put away at night), six kinder-garten tables, 24 small chairs in oak, two Principals..... and just three pupils.

Westholme School now has 1,050 pupils (aged 3-18 years) on three separate sites (Lower, Middle and Upper School) and the facilities and academic reputation which have taken it to its present position as a leading Girls' Independent School. Whether in economically good years or bad, through war or in peace time, the school has grown. By 1926, Miss Singleton had 40 pupils. They had outgrown the single class-room and so she moved to 'Westholme', her family house at 167 Preston New Road and so gave her school its name. By 1929 though, this, too, was insufficient; there was no hall and there wasn't enough space for games. Miss Richmond, although only in her twenties, had 'retired'. She had become engaged and married women could not teach, so Miss Singleton, now sole Principal, employed an assistant teacher and looked around for another

property. In 1930, the perfect place came on the market, Billinge House, the infant department of Blackburn Girls' High School.

She moved in with her children and told the parents in her next prospectus that it provided the best modern facilities: central heating, radio, gramophone, lantern and kinematograph apparatus - and space for games. For the next twenty years the school increased steadily in numbers and was recognised as 'efficient' by the Board of Education in 1940. This was an honour accorded to just ten preparatory schools in the whole of Lancashire; three of them were in Blackburn. The trouble with being a recognised Preparatory School, though, was that pupils aged thirteen and above would have to leave and they didn't want to; they liked it.

Miss Singleton consulted the school inspectors whose answer was unequivocal: to have a senior department, another building would have to be found. It looked as if Westholme would be on the move again.

By now though, Miss Singleton was ready to retire and she would have to sell her school. She found a

Rouse had given his name to another classroom block and the School once again announced its 'final stage of expansion' through *The Lancashire Evening Telegraph* .... but Wilmar Lodge Farm came on the market. Westholme seized the opportunity to turn the land it stood on into the school's playing fields and to convert the farm itself into a Sixth Form Centre.

By the time of the appointment of the current Principal, Mrs Lillian Croston, BSc Hons (Dunelm), PGCE, ALCM, in 1988, the School's results at A level and GCSE were beginning to make the headlines. Places at universities including Oxford and Cambridge became the norm for leavers.

remarkable buyer. Arthur Rouse had returned from fighting on the Normandy Beaches with the South Lancashire Regiment to his wife in Warrington to resume his occupation as a teacher. Together they became Westholme's next Principals, and set about solving the problem of keeping the senior girls. In 1953 they bought 'Garth' on St Silas' Road. Fifty three of the older girls moved there with Mrs Rouse as Headteacher and in 1956 the Senior Department was also 'recognised'. This turned out to be a temporary site as in 1957 Mr and Mrs Rouse bought Beardwood Bank which had two netball courts, five classrooms, a laboratory for Biology and plenty of space for 100 girls. At the time it seemed as if they now had reached the final stage of expansion. By 1967, though, the school was once again full! Financing the next ambitious move would be complex. Mr Rouse sold the school to the Parents to be administered by a Board of Governors. To raise money for the expansion they asked parents and friends to lend the school money. Mr Ian Woolley, a former pupil, who was to be Chairman of Governers, described this as an 'act of faith'; money was raised simply because the parents believed Westholme had a bright future. They were right. The sum realised allowed them to buy Wilmar Lodge on Meins Road which became the Senior or 'Upper' School. Mr Rouse remained as Principal based at Billinge House and Dr Bond, Senior Lecturer at Salford University, was appointed Headteacher of the Senior School in 1968, later becoming Principal herself when Mr Rouse retired.

With several acres to play with at Wilmar Lodge, expansion was immediately on the cards. The first stage was the multi-purpose Clitheroe Hall, then, in October 1970, the 'Thatcher Wing' was opened by the future Prime Minister. The Sports Hall, Swimming Pool, Library Wing and an Art Block swiftly followed for by now there were 475 pupils in the Upper School alone.

By the early eighties computers were installed, Mr

Science was increasingly popular so six custom-made laboratories for Biology, Chemistry and Physics were opened in 1994 by Dr Helen Sharman, OBE, Britain's first astronaut.

Most recently Westholme's new Theatre and Assembly Hall was unveiled. It seats seven hundred and has the latest technology including computer-controlled lighting and rectractable seating. It also has several hundred performers. With concerts, plays and musicals regular features of school life, it never knows a dull moment.

Over the past seventy five years Westholme has changed its buildings and its facilities beyond recognition but it has not changed its name nor the 'act of faith' that places its pupils at the centre of a bright future.

Top left: Helen Sharman, Britain's first astronaut opened Westholme School's £1.25m science and technology wing in July 1994. *Above:* Westholme's superb new Theatre and Assembly Hall. *Facing page, top left:* Miss Singleton, the founder, is pictured on the left with some of her pupils (1926 - 1930). *Facing page, top right:* A 1950s picture of Billinge House. *Facing page, centre left:* The School's first prospectus (1923 - 1926).
Facing page, bottom: P.E. in the 1950s.

ACKNOWLEGMENTS

THE PUBLISHERS WOULD LIKE TO THANK THE FOLLOWING ORGANISATIONS FOR ALLOWING REPRODUCTION OF THEIR PHOTOGRAPHS WITHIN THIS BOOK:

BLACKBURN MUSEUM

BLACKBURN LOCAL STUDIES LIBRARY

THE LANCASHIRE EVENING TELEGRAPH

HOWARD TALBOT

PHOTOGRAPH COMPILATION/COVER DESIGN.....................................MARK SMITH
CAPTIONS RESEARCH AND COMPILATION......................................PHIL HOLLAND
DESIGNERS...MANDY WALKER & NICKY BRIGHTON
COPYWRITER...PAULINE BELL
BUSINESS DEVELOPMENT EDITOR...ANDREW HALES